Comeback

Fred.

Comeback

Overcoming the Setbacks in Your Life

Rick McDaniel

WestBow
PRESS
A DIVISION OF THOMAS NELSON

WestBow Press books may be ordered through booksellers or by contacting:

WestBow Press
A Division of Thomas Nelson
1663 Liberty Drive
Bloomington, IN 47403
www.westbowpress.com
1-(866) 928-1240

ISBN: 978-1-4497-4126-6 (sc)
ISBN: 978-1-4497-4125-9 (hc)
ISBN: 978-1-4497-4127-3 (e)

Library of Congress Control Number: 2012903228

Printed in the United States of America

WestBow Press rev. date: 3/05/2012

To my sons Matt and Wes:
Even though you are young men,
you already know comebacks are possible.

Acknowledgments

I am blessed with many great people in my life. The staff at Richmond Community Church supports me as I pursue sharing God's message with a larger audience. Maria Harwood has helped me work with WestBow/Thomas Nelson Publishers. Matt McGhan has produced the perfect cover for this book. My wife, Michelle, continues to encourage me to follow my dreams.

Contents

Introduction

Comebacks are possible; in fact, they happen all the time. Yet, if you have had a setback, a comeback may seem impossible to you. This book is about the reality of a comeback, and that it can begin for you today. If you are willing to put into practice the principles in this book, you will overcome the setback in your life. You can have an incredible comeback!

I live in Richmond, Virginia, and we had a front row seat to one of the best comebacks in recent memory. Virginia Commonwealth University had ended their 2011 college basketball season poorly. The team lost five of their last eight games and finished fourth in the Colonial Athletic Association. They did do well in the conference tournament but lost in the championship game. The program was successful in recent years, so this was certainly a setback. They did not have high hopes for making the NCAA tournament, so they did not even gather together as a team on Selection Sunday.

But they were selected amidst much controversy, having to play in one of the newly created play-in games. The VCU basketball team decided a comeback was in order. They reeled off five straight wins in the tournament against highly ranked teams, including number-one seed Kansas and ended up making the Final Four. VCU had never made the Final Four and considering the ending to their season, this was a comeback for the ages (at least in Richmond).

Apple is one of the most profitable and highly regarded companies in the world; it is hard to imagine a company that is doing better or has a brighter future. The 2001 release of the iPod has changed how people listen to music, the 2007 release of the iPhone has changed how people use cellular phones, and the 2010 release of the iPad is changing how people use all forms of media. These impressive products sell at phenomenal rates, and this is on top of Apple's line of personal computers that has a very loyal customer base. Yet in 1997, Apple was on the verge of bankruptcy. Apple was in desperate need of a comeback, so Steve Jobs returned to the company and lead them from setback to comeback.

The Los Angeles Lakers won back-to-back NBA championships in 2009 and 2010, but not too long ago, things were much different in Tinsel Town. In 2006 and 2007, the Lakers lost in the playoffs, and their star, Kobe Bryant, was ready to leave the team. Those setbacks brought Bryant to the lowest depths of disappointment in his career. The discouraging defeats lead the Lakers to make roster changes and redouble their intensity that resulted in their comeback championship seasons.

Our entire country has experienced an economic setback. The impact of what has happened is unprecedented in our generation. Declines in consumer spending, which occurred in 2008 and 2009, were the first consecutive declines since the 1930s. Since World War II, annual consumption spending had only fallen twice before in 1974 and 1980. Unemployment is at levels not seen in over a generation. We need a massive financial comeback. Two hundred and eighty thousand jobs need to be added each month for the next five years to get us back to pre-recession employment levels. But an economic recovery is faltering. Though there are many technical explanations, the recovery comes down to psychology. Only if Americans believe in a comeback can it happen—the recovery is a creature of consumer confidence.

An individual comeback is what this book is ultimately about. There are many incredible, inspiring examples in the chapters to come. But one of the most recent is Michael Vick. He was a fantastic college football player who almost singlehandedly led Virginia Tech to the national championship game. His pro career with the Atlanta Falcons was not as successful, but certainly he was one of a few true game-changing players in the NFL. His personal fortune grew exponentially, as he had a huge contract plus lucrative endorsements, especially with sports powerhouse Nike. Yet the discovery of a dog-fighting ring that he financed and sponsored landed him in prison. He spent eighteen months in prison and more than that time away from football. When he was released from prison, he signed on with the Philadelphia Eagles (the only NFL team that offered him a contract) as a backup quarterback, and many questioned whether he would ever again be successful. But in 2010, Vick not only became the Eagles starting QB, but he also led them to the NFC East title.

So comebacks are possible—even probable—with the right information. If you are ready for *your* comeback, let's go!

CHAPTER 1

REASONS FOR A SETBACK

Life is full of setbacks. You cannot avoid them, no matter what you do, no matter who you are; even Tiger Woods and Lindsay Lohan know that. You can, however, avoid taking a step back when obstacles come. The challenge is knowing how you can overcome your setback.

How do you overcome a job loss?
How do you overcome health issues?
How do you overcome divorce?
How do you overcome financial problems?
How do you overcome the loss of a loved one?

How do you take a setback and make a comeback?

In 2001, *Sports Illustrated* published an article entitled, "Bouncing Back Big Time" where they listed their Top Ten Comebacks of all Time. You would think the comebacks would all have been sports related, but they were not. In fact, the article listed Elvis Presley when he had his television special in 1968 and how that was the beginning of his comeback in popularity. The article talked about how President Truman beat Thomas Dewey in the 1948 presidential election when Dewey was favored in all the polls. Some newspapers had already printed that Dewey was the new president, but Truman made a great comeback, winning the presidency. The article also mentioned Japan and Germany making great comebacks from their World War II defeats, reviving their economies and regaining their world-leader status. However, sports comebacks were included, of course, listing Michael Jordan returning to basketball after retirement and his baseball career to win more championships and Muhammad Ali coming back after several years out of boxing to take back the heavyweight title.

THE GREATEST COMEBACK OF ALL TIME

All of those comebacks were not their number-one comeback of all time however. *Sports Illustrated* said that the top comeback of all time was Jesus Christ's resurrection from the dead.

It was a great victory—the ultimate victory.

From the ultimate setback of death, Jesus came back to life and proved his victory over death. If you doubt the veracity of Jesus' resurrection, consider some evidence. In ancient courts, a woman could not be a witness; only the testimony of a man was accepted. Yet the first witnesses of Jesus' resurrection were women. If it were just a fanciful story, why would the gospel writers have used women as witnesses?

The resurrection cannot be a myth because it does not fit the characteristics of a myth. Myths are developed over time, but the story of Jesus' resurrection was written within twenty years of its happening and was known orally many years before that. Also, Christians never venerated the site of Jesus' death. Rather, they focused on the tomb where he had arisen. In addition, there were approximately five hundred witnesses who saw Jesus after his resurrection. How could that many people all have the story wrong?

The reality is, Jesus was raised from the dead, and because of Jesus' victory over death and sin, we can experience forgiveness and eternal life. We can overcome any setback through the strength God gives. You can make any comeback with the power that is available through Jesus Christ.

Though comebacks are absolutely possible, it is important to understand and identify the reasons for your setback. You must begin with the setback before you can get to the comeback.

You have to understand and identify what caused your setback.

There are numerous potential causes for setbacks, but I believe there are only a few main reasons for setbacks. It is absolutely essential for you to understand what those reasons are because, before you can launch a comeback, you need to understand why you had the setback in the first place.

We need a comeback as a country. The idea to write a book on comebacks first started percolating in my mind last summer as I was thinking about how much America needs to come back from its financial collapse and all the problems it has created. I also thought about the challenges that exist in people's lives that point to the need for a comeback. If you don't need a comeback today, you will at some point. You can never get too far away from the setbacks of life.

WE EXPERIENCE UNEXPECTED CIRCUMSTANCES

So what are these reasons for a setback? The first reason is this: We experience unexpected circumstances. We need look no further than the devastating earthquake in Haiti.

The people of Haiti have had all kinds of problems and challenges throughout the years, but one thing they have not had to deal with is earthquakes. They have dealt with hurricanes. They have dealt with enormous political issues and many other systemic issues in their culture and in their government. But it had been two hundred years since they had an earthquake that caused significant damage. Now this country has suffered a horrific earthquake in, of all places, the most populated area of the entire country— the capital city.

We in America are also experiencing an unexpected circumstance called the Great Recession. Who saw it coming? There are a lot of smart people who have graduate degrees in finance, whose life's work is to monitor the economy, yet they missed it. They didn't see it coming. How is it that we fell into such an unprecedented financial challenge as the one we face today? You may have lost your job and never saw it coming. If you thought there was going to be a problem, you never thought it would be as bad as it has become.

Unexpected circumstances will come into your life. But although unexpected, it is still very important to not *dwell* on them but *acknowledge* them. Some of you may have trouble admitting, "Yeah, I've had a setback," or "I'm in the middle of a setback." But you don't have to take a step back because you've had a setback. You can take your setback and turn it into a comeback. However, it is important to acknowledge the setback, and be honest with yourself about your situation.

When the NFL named Tom Brady as its *Comeback Player of the Year*, I was blown away. The guy who has had more success in professional football than anyone else over the last several years is now the Comeback Player of the Year. He has won three Super Bowl championships and has set the record for most touchdowns ever thrown in one season. How could Tom Brady be Comeback Player of the Year? How could someone that good *need* a comeback? Well, when someone lands on your knee in the wrong way and you miss an entire season because of injury, you need a comeback. Sometimes things happen that are unexpected.

I will never forget when one of the men in our church came to me a number of years ago and said, "Pastor Rick, I need to talk to you, and I need to talk to you right now."

"Okay," I said. "What's going on?"

"I came home from a business trip, and my wife was gone."

"What do you mean, 'gone'?"

"I mean her stuff is gone, and she's gone. I've called her, and there is no answer."

I asked him if he had seen this coming, and he said he had not. They were newly married. He thought everything was fine, but apparently it was not.

Life has a way of throwing you curveballs. You go to the doctor. You think you just have a little something wrong. They do a few tests, and the result is totally unexpected. Now you find yourself in a completely different place in life. Unexpected circumstances happen.

Even if circumstances are beyond your control, you can still control your comeback. You can control how you will launch yourself out of the setback and into the comeback, and that is very important to understand at the setback stage.

It is so crucial to understand that you have to acknowledge the setback, but you don't have to accept it. Instead, you look forward to the comeback. We won't allow unexpected circumstances—things that are beyond our control—to dictate to us what our future is going to be. We decide what our life is going to be like, the happiness that we are going to have, and that a comeback will happen.

WE MAKE BAD DECISIONS

There is another reason why we experience setbacks: We make bad decisions—sometimes ones we can't get around. Proverbs 14:8–12 says:

> Wise people have enough sense to find their way, but stupid fools get lost. Fools don't care if they are wrong, but God is pleased when people do right. No one can really know how sad or happy you are. The tent of a good person stands longer than the house of someone evil. You may think you are on the right road and still end up dead.

What Proverbs is saying is that we need wisdom to understand life's challenges, as wisdom is knowledge applied to life.

> "Fools don't care if they are wrong, but God is pleased when people do right."

We can make decisions that end up being wrong, and we have to acknowledge that. We can't go around pretending our foolish decisions haven't caused a setback. It's disappointing and very humbling, but it shouldn't keep us from owning the reason for our setback.

Sometimes, when you don't take care of yourself physically, you end up at the doctor. A logical progression of not taking care of the body God has given you is that you end up with a health setback. Health problems can be unexpected, but many are not because of circumstances within your control. You could have controlled them, but you decided not to.

I think a great way to learn control when it comes to diet is to fast. There are many good reasons for fasting.

One reason is, Jesus told us to fast. He did not say *if* you fast, He said *when* you fast (Matthew 6:16.)

A second reason for fasting is that you will have spiritual experiences like you won't have in any other way.

And third, fasting will bring blessing and favor into your life in a special way.

It is also helpful to understand why God chose fasting. The desire for food is natural, normal, and powerful, so giving up food helps you to understand the influence that it has over your life. Seeing some of the choices you make with your diet and the way you use food for comfort is very illuminating.

In 2007, the last year that the data was available, the number-one reason why people filed bankruptcy was because of medical bills. As the Bible says,

> "You may think you are on the right road and still end up dead."

Unexpected circumstances can adversely affect your finances.

After medical bills, the reasons why people have filed bankruptcy and have financial problems are all lumped into the category of bad decisions. This economic downturn was unexpected, but some are suffering because of bad financial decisions they made. Some chose to buy a house that was beyond anything they needed and thus purchased a home that was too much house for too much money. Others made decisions to live beyond their means, used credit cards to purchase what they wanted, and then found themselves in way too much debt. Many used their home equity line as free spending; thinking the value of their home would always increase and cover the amount.

Other setbacks, such as divorce, can be the result of bad decision-making. Perhaps you did not go through premarital counseling, or you did not take enough time to get to know the person before you made what is supposed to be a lifelong commitment. Or you may have ignored the advice of your parents and friends.

You will never make a comeback until you first acknowledge the setback and then your responsibility in making the bad decision in the first place.

WE FAIL TO PLAN

There is another reason for a setback: We fail to plan. You know the motto, "When you fail to plan, you plan to fail." Look again at what the Bible says,

> "Wise people have enough sense to find their
> way, but stupid fools get lost."

You may say, "I don't know if I like the Bible calling me stupid." Well, sometimes the truth hurts.

People who are wise have a plan,
Have a path,
Have a direction!

And when you don't, you can find yourself suffering a setback.

You have a setback because you didn't know where you were going, and then you wonder, "Why am I here?" You have got to face that your lack of planning has now created a setback in your life. Without a plan, you are adrift, and then you open yourself up to continual setbacks in your life.

When Henry Ford built the first automobile, he forgot to include a reverse gear. It was an incredible invention that has changed our world forever, but you can't always drive forward. But Henry bounced back; he added a reverse gear, and then things went very well for him and his car company. Like Henry Ford, you too can bounce back from your lack of planning. But it is absolutely crucial to understand the importance of direction and planning. And that is what makes following Christ so valuable.

To have a comeback without God's help is much more difficult. If you follow Him, you have a built-in plan for your life, which makes life so much easier and simpler. You are then able to understand His purpose and plan for your life. As a matter of fact, following Jesus is a continuous unfolding of God's plan for your life.

God has a plan unique for you; it is not like anyone else's in the world. In order to discover it, you must follow Him. He will then take you places, both expected and unexpected—a marvelous ride that wards off setbacks. There are enough unexpected things that happen in life, so we don't need to make it any harder. We no longer need to cooperate with the challenges of life. If we plan and follow God's plan, we will find ourselves far ahead of the game.

WE IGNORE GOD'S INSTRUCTIONS

Another reason for setbacks: We ignore God's instructions. What does the Bible say?

> "The tent of a good person stands longer than
> the house of someone evil."

When you follow God's instructions, you will not do evil.

The Bible is our owner's manual for life. I recently had a problem with one of my cars. I looked up the section in the owner's manual that dealt with the problem and did what it said to do. Because I followed the instructions, I avoided a potentially costly repair. Some don't like to use the owner's manual, though, because they think they can figure things out for themselves.

This is how some of you have gotten into the setback you are currently in because you are not following the Manual, the Bible. Meanwhile, the people who are following the Bible's instructions are avoiding setbacks. They are reading the number-one bestseller of all time and taking advantage of the greatest wealth of wisdom available. But if you don't follow its instructions, you can end up in a setback position. Then you have to get real with yourself and acknowledge your responsibility. When you don't obey God, when you go against his teachings, you end up in a setback.

Neil White tells his story in the book, *In the Sanctuary of Outcasts*. His setback involved losing his business and ending up in prison for check fraud. But the Louisiana prison he went to was not an ordinary prison; it was the last home in the United States for people disfigured by leprosy. Yet even though he had gone bankrupt, left thirty of his employees without jobs, cost bankers a million dollars, and betrayed his wife and children, he still did not acknowledge his wrongdoing. Not until he was in a sanctuary for outcasts who could not hide their disfigurement could he see his own. His desire to be successful and admired had caused him to ignore the reality that he was a thief. Though his disfigurement was on the inside, he still needed to accept that his stealing caused his setback. He had ignored his own morals and religious teachings; only by seeing the truth, which he finally did, was he able to make a comeback.

If you are going to have a comeback, you must follow God's principles. If you want to avoid a setback, you must follow God's instructions, which is not advice that you can take or leave. God's principles are the way to live your life, and following God's instructions is the way your life will turn out for the best, and God's plan for you will be fulfilled. This is how you can have happiness and peace.

It is not enough to know the principles; you must do something more—you must put them into practice. And when you do, you will avoid setbacks.

YOU CAN AVOID SETBACKS

You can avoid setbacks in life—not all, but many. You can recognize and understand the reasons why you have setbacks. The Bible says,

> "Fools don't care if they are wrong!"

If you don't care, get used to a life of setbacks and disappointment. But I don't think you want that or you would not be reading this book.

Sometimes we have setbacks, and when we do, we need to identify the reason why, which is the beginning of a marvelous comeback in our lives. The setback doesn't mean we have to take a step back, nor does it mean we have to stay in the setback position.

You are now in position to have a marvelous comeback.

CHAPTER 2

LESSONS FROM A SETBACK

There is a man from Richmond, Virginia, named John Kuester, a high school basketball star who received a scholarship to the University of North Carolina. After his basketball-playing days were over, he entered into the field of coaching. By the age of twenty-seven, he had his first head coaching job at Boston University, where he coached for a couple of years before going on to George Washington University and coaching for another five years. But when he was thirty-five, he had a losing season and got fired. For the first time in his life, John was without a job. In an interview with John O'Conner in the *Richmond Times-Dispatch* he says this about it,

"I was unemployed and wondering what I should do. I had two avenues to go. One was to look to do something different for an occupation. The other was to get better at my craft of being a coach."

John got hired by the Boston Celtics, but not as a coach. After a number of years, he eventually became a key assistant coach. In 2009, at the age of fifty-four, John got another opportunity to be a head coach, this time with the Detroit Pistons. Here is what he says about his experience,

"You are going to have setbacks. But how are you going to handle those things and learn from them? You need to learn from those kinds of situations and that is what I did."

John had a setback, turned it around, had a comeback, and now has a prestigious job. How did that happen? He learned the lessons from his setback.

Before the comeback, you have to look closely at the setback.

A setback should be dissected, not discarded.
Yet many want to discard the setback.

They want to pretend it never happened and move on. No one wants to relive the disappointment, the failure, and the shortcoming of a setback.

LOOK FOR THE LESSON

In order to have a comeback, you must look for the lesson. Many try to push the setback behind them as quickly as possible, which is precisely why so many go from setback to setback to setback. I believe God's desire is for everyone to have a comeback. But in order to do so, there are certain things you must do. And if you are unwilling to look for the lessons in the setback, you will never enjoy a comeback.

Some want to point their finger at God and say, "You've done me wrong. You never bless me; I never end up on the right side of things." The reality is, before you turn away from or blame God for the setback, you need to ask yourself if God is trying to tell you something. Ecclesiastes 10:8–10 says:

> If you dig a pit, you might fall in. If you break down a wall, a snake might bite you. You could even get hurt by chiseling a stone or chopping a log. If you don't sharpen your ax, it will be harder to use. If you are smart, you will know what to do.

If you are smart, you will ask yourself, "Is there a lesson here?" Maybe there is, or maybe God is trying to show you something.

Before you run away from or try to bury it,
before you try to stop thinking about it,
remember that God may have gotten your attention for a reason.

The setback is so that you might sharpen your ax and be smarter the next time.

There are stupid people, and there are smart people. What's the difference? It is not IQ. Actually the Bible's definition isn't about innate intelligence. When the Bible talks about smart or stupid, it is referring to wisdom, which is the application of knowledge.

All of us can receive knowledge that we can either apply or not. The Bible says if you are smart, you will know what to do. You will know that you need to be careful when you are chiseling a stone or when you are chopping down a tree. You need to be wise about the things you do. And if you hurt yourself the first time, you will make sure to learn the lesson for the next time. But you need to look for the lesson. Whatever has happened, whatever your setback may be, you need to look for the lesson. If you think there is no lesson, you need to look harder and peer deeper.

A couple will come to me and say, "We want to get married. We have both been divorced and have fallen in love, so we want to get remarried." I have a premarital process I use with couples to properly prepare them for a lifelong commitment, but the reality is that sixty percent of second marriages end in divorce. What is going on?

People are not looking for the lesson. They are not looking for what they can learn from their first failed marriage that will keep them from experiencing the same setback again. If you failed the first time, you want to make sure it does not happen a second time.

You can blame other people.
You can think it is just bad luck.
You can try to not think about it at all.

Or you can look for the lesson.

A good approach would be to ask, "Is there anything I can take away from this setback?"

You lost your job. Is it downsizing, or the economy? Maybe, maybe not. It could be when it came time to downsize; there was a process and a choice to be made. Maybe you didn't keep up your skills the way you should have. Possibly you were hard to work with, or you did not work hard enough. This is hard stuff to look at, but you need to look for the lesson.

There was a man named Wallace Johnson, who you probably never heard of. Sixty years ago when he was forty years old, he got fired from his job. When he told his wife, she said, "What are we going to do now?" He said, "I want to take a mortgage out on our home. I want to get money together and start my own construction company." Within five years, he was making a lot of money. He says this: "At the time it happened, I didn't understand why I was fired. Later, I saw that it was God's wondrous plan for me. It was God's plan for me to get me onto a different path and a different way."

You may not know who Wallace Johnson is, but you may have heard of the company he founded—Holiday Inn. By the time he passed away, he was a multimillionaire.

THERE ARE MANY DIFFERENT LESSONS

God can do amazing things and bring about marvelous comebacks, but first you must uncover the lesson from the setback. You thought you had arrived, and possibly that is what happened to you. You got to a place of success where you didn't care how you treated other people, or you didn't care about certain decisions you made because you had "arrived."

> There is the lesson of the whale: "Just when you get to the top and you start to blow, you can get harpooned."

Maybe you are a fearful person. You got afraid and anxious and didn't want to take the necessary risks. Maybe the lesson for you is to stop letting fear dictate your life and future. Stop making fear-based decisions, and start making faith-based decisions.

Or your setback may be that you quit.

You decided that you could not keep going,
That things were too difficult,
So you simply gave up.

The lesson for you is to persevere through the difficulties. Keep at it, because eventually you will succeed. For everyone who has a setback, there are lessons to be learned.

I read on *msnbc.com* about a woman named Lucia Del Barto from Arizona, who shared what has happened to her in this current recession. She said, "If it weren't for the economy going so bad, I'd still be blowing money left and right and not even trying to better myself with an education. I'm grateful because of the recession. The recession gave me a new opportunity, hope, and purpose."

Not many people are thanking God for the recession. Yet here is a woman who sees the recession as a wakeup call to look for the lesson. And for her the lesson was to stop blowing money and to get an education, thus providing a more solid and secure foundation for her future.

LEARN FROM THE LESSON

God can use the tough, difficult, and challenging experiences of life for your good if you are willing to look for the lesson. But many people want to throw the lessons aside or brush them off rather than face them head-on and ask the hard questions. "Is there a lesson here for me in this setback? What is it I can learn from this?" You should be looking for the lesson in your setback, and you need to learn that lesson.

It is one thing to look for the lesson,
But it is another thing to actually learn from it.

Despite setbacks, you can learn from them. And in learning from them, you can fashion a marvelous comeback.

I love Walt Disney. I have read a number of biographies about him. He fascinates me for his creative energy and marvelous visionary leadership. What you might not know is that he experienced seven very disappointing setbacks in his life. But Walt Disney always looked for the lesson and learned from the lesson. Therefore, he didn't repeat his mistakes. When you think of him, you think of the movies and the theme parks. His name is on a television and a radio network. The Disney name is the gold standard for creativity.

The lesson means nothing if we don't learn it and make the appropriate change. You don't need to wonder why so many people never have a comeback: It is because they are unwilling to learn the lesson.

Warren Buffett, one of the richest people in the world, often talks about one of his early setbacks when he was not accepted into Harvard. He says, "Setbacks teach lessons that carry you along. You learn that a temporary defeat is not a permanent one. In the end, it can be an opportunity." Buffett used what he learned from his setback early in life to become an incredible financial success.

LEARN FROM THE GREAT RECESSION

Since this great recession has caused so much financial challenge, it might be worthwhile to look at the possible lessons to be learned.

What can we learn from the experience that we have been through? I think the first thing we can learn is to live within our means. If you live within your means, you don't get into debt. And if you don't get into debt, you won't find yourself so negatively impacted by the loss of a job or a decrease in your income.

For a number of years, some folks were buying homes that were beyond what they even needed—for example, a four thousand-square-foot home with five bedrooms for a family of four. A good way to know you are buying a house that is too big for you is when you can't even furnish it. If they had purchased the three thousand-square-foot, four-bedroom house, it could have cost $150,000 less. And it is that extra money each month for the mortgage that is causing financial hardship. Live within your means; that is a good lesson to learn.

Debt can be very destructive. Having an extra payment or payments every month limits you financially. Instead of investing or saving money, you have to pay your debts, and the amount of interest you pay can be more than your original debt. The pressure and stress that debt places on you is simply not worth it. Getting out and staying out of debt frees you up financially, so a financial setback will not destroy you.

Here is another lesson: Know your financial basics. Too many people do not know basic financial principles necessary to succeed. These basics include having a budget, debt reduction, investing, real estate, insurance, and giving. Having basic knowledge on home mortgages (interest rates, closing costs, fixed versus adjustable rates, etc.) could have spared thousands from unwise home purchases that have created a huge financial setback for so many. Knowing your financial basics can help you navigate through challenging times and avoid a painful setback.

What other lessons can we learn? That nothing lasts forever. Prices for real estate can go up and up, but eventually they come down. The stock market can rocket to record levels, but a correction will eventually lower it. Growth is great, but nothing grows forever. McDonalds had twenty-five years where they increased their profits each year, one hundred successive quarters of increasing profits, but eventually even that ended.

It is foolish to think we can experience only good financial times and never have setbacks. Good times never last forever, and neither do the bad. Learn the lessons.

DON'T MAKE THE SAME MISTAKES AGAIN

Learn the lesson so you don't repeat the same mistake. You may not want to revisit your setback. Everything in you may never want to think about it again, but you need to look for the lesson or lessons. You need to learn. You don't want to go through the same pain again, and you don't have to. You don't need to repeat the same mistakes again. You can learn so you can go from the setback to the comeback. Put into practice the wisdom that you have learned through defeat and failure. Use the knowledge and the feedback to forge

A better way to go,
A better route to take,
A better path to your future.

Suppose you make a big mistake on your job. How do you regain credibility from your setback? You own up to your mistake. If you are at fault, don't make excuses or take a defensive stance. Go to your boss and share the lessons you have learned from the experience. If you can make amends or correct the mistake, do it. If you cannot do anything to change the situation, take responsibility for putting a process into place to undo the damage if possible and keep the mistake from happening again.

Rod Blagojevich, the former governor of Illinois, has experienced quite a setback. He has been convicted of seventeen counts in a corruption case involving his role in filling the open Senate seat of Barack Obama. Blagojevich has gone from being governor to a convicted felon. He had these poignant words to say after his conviction, "Among the many lessons that I've learned from this whole experience is to try to speak a little bit less."

Psalm 34:17 says,

> "When his people pray for help, he listens and
> rescues them from their troubles. The Lord is
> there to rescue all who are discouraged and

have given up hope. The Lord's people may suffer a lot, but he will always bring them safely through."

Here is the good news: God will help you. He will bring you from a setback to a comeback. "The Lord's people may suffer a lot, but he will always bring them safely through." After you have looked for the lesson and learned from it, after you have done your part, here is what God says to you:

"I will help you.
I will rescue you.
I will bring you from a setback to a comeback."

That is God's message to you. That is the God we serve. If you don't have a relationship with God, this is one of the reasons why you want to have one with him through Jesus Christ. If you have a relationship with God, you can stand on the promise that God takes you from setbacks to comebacks.

God wants us to pause long enough to look for the lesson in the setback. He wants us to take enough time to learn the lessons we need to learn so we don't experience yet another setback. Then we can move in God's direction for our lives—a positive, growing, uplifting direction God wants for each of us.

When President Obama gave the State of the Union address, he said, "We've had some setbacks as a country." He then said, "I've had some setbacks." That is an acknowledgment of reality that is true for all of us in some way. Now the question is, "How are we going to have a comeback?"

The comeback will happen because of change. Things have to be different. If you want to have a comeback, you have to be willing to change. You have to be willing to do things different from what you've done up to this point. Being ready for a comeback means you are ready to change.

There is a fascinating comeback story in the Bible, but it is a somewhat unknown comeback story because you have to dig to find it. The story is about a man named Mark, recorded in Mark 14:50–52:

> "All of Jesus' disciples ran off and left him. One of them was a young man who was wearing only a linen cloth. And when the men grabbed him, he left the cloth behind and ran away naked."

The next part of the story is found in the book of Acts 13:13:

> "Paul and the others left Paphos and sailed to Perga, which is in Pamphylia. But John left them and went back to Jerusalem."

The final part of the story is found in 2 Timothy 4:11:

"Only Luke has stayed with me. Mark can be very helpful to me, so please find him and bring him with you."

Mark also went by his first name, John. Acts 12:12 says

"When this dawned on him, he went to the house of Mary, the mother of John, also called Mark."

Some people go by their middle name not their first name and John Mark did this. We discovered my eldest son did this as well. He is named Matthew Graham and we have always called him Matt. When he went away to college at West Point there were so many Matt's that he decided to be called by Graham. When we went to one of his first football games people were talking to us about "Graham" and my wife and I were looking at each other wondering whom they were talking about. After the game we asked our son and he told us that at West Point he is called Graham.

So John Mark wrote the gospel of Mark, which tells us something that the gospels of Matthew, Luke, and John don't. Only in Mark are we told that there was a young man who ran away naked when Jesus was arrested. Since Mark included that information in his gospel without naming himself, we can deduce that the naked guy who fled was Mark.

USELESS TO USEFUL

We are introduced to Mark initially in the book of Acts as a coward. When things get tough, he runs. He is such a coward that even when people grab him and his clothes, he runs away, leaving his clothes behind. Years later, we are reintroduced to this guy again in Acts 13:5,

> "When they arrived at Salamis, they proclaimed the word of God in the Jewish synagogues. John was with them as their helper."

Now he is called John. Sometimes he is called Mark, sometimes he is called John, but it is the same guy—John Mark.

The story here is that two men named Paul and Barnabas are going on a missionary journey. By the way, Barnabas and (John) Mark are cousins. They are going into dangerous territories, and if you were to read the rest of chapter 13, you would see the kind of danger they encountered. Paul and Barnabas leave, and Mark comes along as their helper, their assistant. Just a few verses later, in Acts 13:13, we read,

> "John Mark left them and went back to Jerusalem."

So fifteen years earlier Mark was a coward, who fled, leaving Jesus behind. Now, in a new endeavor with his cousin Barnabas and Paul, he quits again when things get tough.

He was a coward before, and now he is also a quitter. These are setbacks, major setbacks in this young man's life.

We read in 1 Peter 5:13,

> "So does my son Mark."

Ten years later, the apostle Peter considers Mark to be like a son to him. So something has happened. The coward and the quitter had quite a comeback. He is now seen by one of the great leaders of the early church as someone so valuable that he is like a son to him. In fact, the gospel of Mark, although written by Mark, is actually Peter's eyewitness account of the life of Jesus. Peter spent three years with Jesus and then shared all his knowledge with Mark who wrote it as one of the gospels.

Then in Colossians 4:10, the same Paul who Mark quit on before lists several people as fellow workers with him, "And Mark, one of my fellow workers." The guy who was a coward and a quitter is now considered to be a fellow worker with the apostle Paul. Then 2 Timothy 4:11 says,

> "Only Lucas stayed with me. Mark can be very helpful to me, so please bring him with you."

This man who was a coward and had a setback, was a quitter and had another setback, has now had such a comeback that the apostle Paul believes Mark could be very helpful and wants him brought to Paul.

What happened to this young man? How did he go from terrible setbacks to this marvelous comeback? There is no information in the Bible about how this happened, but here is what I deduce from this story. Something changed in Mark so dramatically that he overcame these terrible setbacks. What could have destroyed a person—"I'm a coward. I walked out on Jesus. I'm such a quitter. I quit on Paul and Barnabas. I have failed, and I have fallen short in so many ways"—did not destroy Mark. He made an incredible comeback. Peter and Paul, the two great leaders of the early church, both believed he was a valuable person.

CHANGE YOUR MIND

An incredible, marvelous change took place in Mark's life. If you are going to go from setback to comeback, there must be a change in your life. And the change must be a change of mind.

A change of mind happens when you receive new information and gain new knowledge. Part of that new knowledge is gained through the setback. We have covered the information in learning the lessons in the previous chapter.

With any new knowledge, there is resistance to changing your mind. I'm in the business of helping people become who God wants them to be, and I've seen this resistance firsthand. The resistance is mostly fear of the unknown. The way you overcome fear is with belief. You believe that the change can happen, that it can be done. You trust that you can be different and that you can be better. You can do it this time because you know more, you are wiser, and you have opened yourself up to the principles that will lead to a comeback.

A few years ago, members of a tribe in South America kept dying prematurely, so some scientists were brought in to find out why. They discovered that the people were getting a specific disease from insects that lived inside the clay adobe walls of their huts. It was great to have this new information, but the question for the tribe was what to do.

One possible solution was they could move to another place where those insects did not live. Thus they would no longer get the disease and no longer die prematurely.

Another possibility was to tear down the existing huts and rebuild them, using an insecticide in the clay that would repel the insects so they would not get into the homes. Thus the huts would no longer make the people sick, and they wouldn't die of the disease.

A third option was to remain the same and continue dying prematurely.

Now of those three options, which one would you opt for? You may not know which of the first two options to choose, but anyone would know the third option is not really an option. To do nothing would mean continued early death, so action needed to be taken. But the South American tribe chose to do nothing. They decided to stay where they were and live in the same huts they lived in.

We can look at those people and think, "Why would they not change?" But before we judge the poor, uneducated tribesmen in another land, we might want to ask ourselves, "What is it *we* are refusing to change?"

How many setbacks do you have to have before you are ready for a comeback? A comeback means change, and the first thing that must change is your mind.

CHANGE YOUR HEART

After a change of mind, there must be a change of heart. A change of heart is the result of a new attitude, when you decide that your way or mode of thinking (which is the definition of an attitude) is going to change. You determine that you are going to see things from a different perspective. When you see things from a different perspective, and you think differently about yourself, others, and God, you then have a change of heart.

It is amazing how you can move from a setback to a comeback when you change your attitude. Some people have never had the comeback they should have had, and the reason is because they refused to change their attitude. A negative attitude will never lead to a comeback. Never.

You may know the name Lee Child. He has written thirteen books, several of them bestsellers. He initially got into the motion picture business and spent the early part of his career doing television and making movies and was very happy.

For fifteen years, Lee worked in a family-owned company where everyone was actually treated like family. But then the company was purchased by a larger company, which happens all the time in business. One of the first things the new owner did was get rid of the original owners and then the employees, which included Lee. He says,

"I was thirty-nine years old and soon to be forty. Not a great age to be unemployed. If there was ever a time to make a change, this was it."

Lee looked at his big setback and decided what he really wanted to do: write novels. So he had to figure out a way to support himself and his family while he wrote. In order to do this, his wife had to go back into the workplace and his teenage daughter had to waitress to help the family get by. In a *Parade* article he goes on to say this,

"The point is this. If you're fired at forty, it's not about the hurt, it's not about the betrayal, it's not about the fear, it's about the opportunity."

That kind of attitude led to his comeback.

Many people have lost their jobs in the recession, but their attitude about it is not one of opportunity. Rather, it is one of never getting as good a job again or making as much money. The setback does involve hurt, anger, and betrayal.

However, if you're going to get out of the setback and into the comeback, it's going to be about your attitude. You need to begin thinking differently. You must open yourself up to new possibilities, new opportunities, and new experiences. But if your attitude doesn't change and you don't have a change of heart, it won't happen.

Mitch Albom tells the story of a man named Tom Smallwood who got laid off from General Motors two days before Christmas in 2008. He applied for other jobs but received no response. He was married, had a one-year-old daughter, and was out of job options. So Tom decided to make a significant change. He would pursue his boyhood dream of becoming a professional bowler.

Tom started going to the bowling alley every day, and in May, he entered the Pro Bowlers Association Tour Trials. He bowled nine games a day for five days, and when it was all over, he had qualified for a tour exemption, which meant a guaranteed spot and a minimum paycheck at each PBA event for a year. He says, "It was like someone said, 'Congratulations, you got a new job.'" Tom saw losing his job as an opportunity to pursue a dream, one he never would have considered had he not lost his job.

But Tom's story does not end there; it gets better. One year after he lost his job with General Motors, he was competing in the PBA World Championship in Wichita, Kansas. He made it all the way to the final, and his opponent was the reigning PBA Player of the Year, Wes "Big Nasty" Malott.

The match came down to the final frame, and Tom threw a strike to win—and he did. He won $50,000, more money than he ever made in one year at his old job.

Tom says about the whole experience,

> "Getting laid off was one of the worst things that ever happened to me. But it led to the best result."

Tom's fantastic comeback was the result of his willingness to change, to think differently, and to explore new opportunities.

CHANGE YOUR FUTURE

There is another change that must happen: You must change your future. But just how do you change your future?

You change your future through commitment.

You change your mind through knowledge,
you change your heart through attitude, and
you change your future through commitment.

You choose to be committed to your comeback.

Everybody wants a comeback, but the difference between people who have setbacks and then comebacks and people who have setbacks and no comebacks is commitment.

You are ready for a comeback when you commit to change. Not when you *want* to change, not when you think you *should* change, and not when you *talk about* changing, but when you *commit* to change. There is a phrase I quote often, "Successful people are simply ordinary people who make commitments others are unwilling to make." I believe that because I have witnessed it over and over again in my life and leadership. When you make commitments, your future changes for the better.

To have a comeback, you simply must be committed to your comeback. You must believe you will have a comeback and stay committed to the process however long it may take. You can change your future, and that change will always involve at its most basic level a willingness to commit. When you commit to do what has to be done to make the changes that need to be made in your life, you are ready for a comeback.

THE GREATEST CHANGE OF ALL

Of all the changes a person could make, one is the preeminent and will lead you to a comeback in your life.

The change is so significant that it is called being born again (John 3:3).

Every person is born physically, and every person needs to be born spiritually, which is what it means to be born again. There has to be a point you come to where you say, "I know I am far from perfect, and a perfect God can't accept an imperfect person like me." You must have enough change of heart to say, "I need God's help in order to become the person I should be. In order to have the comeback I need to have, I must have God's help." And then you must make a commitment, where you say, "God, I commit to following you. I receive your forgiveness through Jesus Christ's death on the cross for my sins. I commit my life to you and to a relationship with you, and I will live my life following your teachings and principles."

This fundamental change is necessary for every person because the Bible says, "All have sinned" (Romans 3:23). No one is perfect; everyone has sinned and fallen short of God's standard. So we all find ourselves in the same human condition. We must come to a place of change, and that foundational change will then guide all our other changes.

Have you ever made that commitment to God? Have you ever had that change experience in your life? If you haven't, here is how it can happen. You pray and tell God your desire for change. Prayer is our way of communicating with God. Pray, "I recognize that I am not perfect, and I know that I need to change. I ask you, Jesus, to come into my life and forgive me of all my past mistakes, failures, and sins. I commit myself to following you as you guide and direct my life. I ask this in your name, Jesus. Amen."

Now you are ready for your comeback.

CHAPTER 4

COMPONENTS OF A COMEBACK

God specializes in do-overs. God specializes in start-overs. God specializes in new beginnings. God specializes in comebacks. If you have had a setback and want a comeback, God is your answer. Zephaniah 3:17 says:

> The Lord your God wins victory after victory and is always with you. He celebrates and sings because of you. And he will refresh your life with his love.

God is always there to bring you to victory.

He celebrates because of you.
He will refresh you.
He will restore you.

Whatever has taken place, whatever the setback in your life, whether financial, the loss of a loved one, a health issue, or a job loss, God wants to bring you to a comeback.

I read in the newspaper about a guy who got shot. When the paramedics brought him into the emergency room, he was still awake and became really scared because the expressions on the faces of the nurses and the doctor told him that he was not going to make it. They asked him, "Are you allergic to anything?" He purposely paused to make sure they were all listening. Then he said, "Bullets. Now operate on me like I'm going to live!" And he did live. This man believed his comeback was possible, and he wanted the people attending to him to believe it too.

Your comeback is possible, but certain key components must exist in your life. When they do, God will do his part.

RESTORE YOUR CONFIDENCE

Will you do your part? Will you do what you can do? If so, the first thing you can do is restore your confidence. You can choose to be confident.

Your confidence always takes a big hit when you have a setback.

When you lose your job, it shakes you. When your spouse walks out the door, it rocks you. Setbacks have a way of affecting your confidence like nothing else, and confidence is crucial to a comeback. Confidence is the expectation that you will succeed and is the power that propels you to a comeback. You have to restore your confidence, your courage, and your edge. People who make comebacks are people who have restored their confidence.

Having confidence should come easier when you know the Bible is telling you that your God is going to win victory after victory and is always with you. You can base your confidence on the reality of who God is.

Confidence helps you to take advantage of new opportunities. Comebacks always come with new opportunities. People who stay in the setback, who allow the setback to become a step back, are people who watch opportunities go by without seizing them. They do not take advantage of these opportunities because they lack confidence. A lack of confidence keeps you from making the decisions you need to make.

Your comeback will be in part about opportunities and the decisions you make about those opportunities. Some people are so negatively impacted by their setbacks that they are paralyzed and cannot make new, better decisions.

David Duval was once the number-one ranked golfer in the world. He had plunged all the way to number 882 and needed to qualify just to play in the 2009 US Open at Bethpage Black. He was tied for the lead on the seventieth hole when his five-foot par putt caught the back of the lip and spun 180 degrees out the other side. He ended up finishing tied for second, his best finish on the PGA tour in eight years. Duval has definitely experienced several setbacks, and I was impressed with his playing so well on such a difficult course in a major championship. But what amazed me most were his comments after the tournament. "I stand before you certainly happy with how I played but extremely disappointed in the outcome. I had no question in my mind I was going to win this golf tournament today." Duval has definitely restored his confidence and is well on his way to a comeback.

Everybody has setbacks; no one is immune. You cannot allow the setback to define you or rob you of your confidence to step into new beginnings and new opportunities. There is a do-over and a start-over for everyone!

God will be with you, but you have to take advantage of those opportunities and act on them. Action comes from confidence, from believing that you can have a comeback. And you absolutely, positively can.

LOSE THE REGRET

Another key component is you must lose the regret. You cannot stay chained to the past. You must refuse to allow the past to determine your ability to have a comeback.

Do not permit guilt and condemnation to ruin your comeback. Don't say,

"If only I had done this.
If only I hadn't done that.
If only I could go back."

The past cannot be changed, but your future certainly can. God's message is restoration, that comebacks are possible with His help. It is the enemy of your soul who wants you to be filled with regret, focused on your past mistakes and failures.

Romans 8:1 says,

> "There is therefore now no condemnation for those who are in Christ Jesus."

If you have received God's forgiveness, there is no guilt. If you haven't, you need to receive that forgiveness.

You cannot change the past, but you can change the negative results of your past actions. You can decide that you will no longer have the same setbacks. Acting with wisdom gained from your setback can eliminate negative results. In the chapter, "Lessons from a Setback," I explained that there are lessons to be learned from a setback. But here is what is important to understand:

You need to learn the lesson and then bury the experience. After you have extracted the lesson from the setback, stop replaying the experience.

I was talking with someone recently about one of my own setbacks. I have learned the lessons, but I have no desire to rehash the experience. Bury the experience. Refuse to allow the hurt, guilt, pain, and disappointment back into your life. Learn the lesson, move on, and lose the regret. Lose the kind of thinking that keeps you stuck in the setback because you can't let go of the past.

You can't make a comeback while dragging around the past. Unfortunately, for many of us, there are people who will not let us forget. It isn't great to have those folks in your life. What I have learned is, either they change or you have to get rid of them. This is not an easy thing to do, but if people keep talking about your past mistakes, they will hinder your comeback.

Refuse to dwell on the past.
Lose the self-pity.
Lose the regret.

You are on your way to a comeback.

HAVE FORWARD FOCUS

A third component of a comeback is having a forward focus. You need to have a laser-like focus, and it must be in a forward direction.

If you focus on your setbacks, you have more setbacks. This is not what God wants for you. It is not God's plan for your life.

You can get past the health challenge,
You will get past this crushing loss,
You will move past the relationship that broke apart.

And you will do so by proceeding with new goals, new vision, for a new future. Your forward focus will not allow you to stay in the setback position any longer.

God creates marvelous comebacks. He does them all the time. Here is a unique comeback story. There was a young couple that wanted to be missionaries to Africa, a very noble desire. As they went through the qualifying process, the wife discovered that she had some medical issues that disqualified her from living in that kind of climate. The couple was devastated. Their dream had died. They longed to serve and help people, but now because of a health issue, they were stopped in their tracks and didn't know what to do.

The young man took over his father's side business in which he made grape juice for communion in church services. He built the business into the huge company that makes Welch's Grape Juice, Welch's Grape Jelly, and many other products, making a lot of money through which he financially supported African missions. This couple never was able to go to Africa, but what a difference they made through their giving. God turned their physical setback into a financial comeback.

You cannot have any more excuses or spend any more time placing blame. Your focus can only be forward. Don't look back. Jesus said,

"No one who puts his hand to the plow and looks back is fit for the kingdom of God"(Luke 9:62).

The kingdom of God is about focusing on the motion that takes you forward. Try balancing a bike just by sitting on it; you can't do it. But if you start moving, you can balance it perfectly. Forward movement—that is the kind of focus that leads to comebacks.

You miss one hundred percent of the shots you never take. You will never see results unless you make an attempt. Do you realize the best shooter makes fifty percent of his shots? If you could shoot fifty percent, you could have a long career playing basketball. That means, half the time you make it, half the time you miss. In baseball, it is even better. If you are a .300 hitter, you can have a long and successful baseball career. A batting average of .300 means that out of ten at bats, you have three hits. It may not seem very impressive to those not familiar with baseball, but it is the standard for a good hitter. If you were to hit .400, you would be in very rare company in the history of baseball.

You must have focus and move forward in the direction of your comeback. If you do not, you will stay in the setback. No one wants to stay in the setback, yet so many people do.

Too many people allow their setback to be a *step* back.

Take one step forward and then another and another by having a laser-like focus on the future that God has planned for you.

REGAIN YOUR MOMENTUM

There is another key component to a comeback: You must regain your momentum. Momentum is one of the best friends you could ever have. A well-known leader once told me, "Rick, momentum is your best friend because momentum will make you better than you could ever be."

Without momentum, you will look worse than you really are which is why setbacks are always about the loss of momentum. When you lose momentum, it is amazing how things can go in the wrong direction. Momentum is so powerful that when you shift from setback to comeback, you can shift the momentum in your life.

It is just as the Bible says—you go from "victory after victory."

Momentum is emerging energy and limitless passion that positively fuels a comeback. What you need is to regain the momentum you once had, and that begins with concrete change and builds through positive experiences. That is how momentum works. You have a positive experience. Then you have another positive experience, which gives you a little more momentum that continues with clear direction, moving you down the path to your comeback. That leads you to a new start, a new beginning, a new goal, a new opportunity, and eventually a new future.

Momentum is mysterious, but I've tried to show how

concrete change + positive experiences + clear direction = momentum.

Momentum is your best friend when you are making a comeback. Nobody has ever had a comeback without it.

Once you get some momentum in your business, job, marriage, family, or health, it is amazing how it will fuel you right into a comeback. It is almost magical how it empowers you. Before you know it, you feel like you are gliding, and things are not so hard. Pieces start falling into place. It is easier to eat better and exercise. It is easier to be married to your spouse, and you start getting along better. You do the things you are supposed to do, and it gets easier. Momentum will fuel you right into a marvelous, powerful comeback.

My youngest son's football team was undefeated in the regular season of his junior year in high school and won the district championship. It was a dream season for a school in only its fourth season of varsity football. They won against teams they had never defeated before in thrilling fashion. My son ran for over eighteen hundred yards and scored twenty-one touchdowns.

They continued to win and went on to play for the regional championship on a bitterly cold night for Virginia, especially in November. They were playing another undefeated team, who was a very formidable opponent.

The game started off great with my son Wes having a long run, scoring a quick touchdown. But from that point on, everything went terribly wrong. They had turnovers, played poorly, and were behind 28–7 at halftime. We held out hope that they could turn it around after halftime, but the other team scored another touchdown, and they were now down 35–7. At that point, the game seemed lost for certain, and their dream season looked to be over.

Then my son's team scored a touchdown. The other team got possession and fumbled the ball. My son's team scored another touchdown, and the other team turned the ball over again. Momentum started kicking in; before we knew it, my son's team had scored four straight touchdowns, and the score was tied.

Each team then kicked a field goal, and the game went into overtime. In high school football, each team has an opportunity to score in overtime. The other team missed a very short field goal, and my son's team made theirs. They had come all the way back from a twenty-eight-point deficit and won the championship, the greatest comeback in Virginia high school football playoff history. The momentum they had in the second half simply propelled them to victory.

You know exactly the comeback you need, that you desire so much. God will be with every person who desires to come out of a setback and into a comeback. If you lose the regret, restore your confidence, and focus on your future, God will propel you into victory after victory. You can ride momentum straight into a comeback.

CHAPTER 5

STEPS TO A COMEBACK

Setbacks don't define you. Everybody has setbacks. You're not a failure because you have setbacks; you are only a failure if you stop trying. I like the words to the Kutless song that says,

> "Impossible is not a word, it's just a reason not to try."

The Bible says what is impossible with man is possible with God (Matthew 19:26). When people say it can't be done, it's an excuse for not trying. I remember these words from Hudson Taylor, a very famous missionary,

> "First, it's impossible. Then, it's difficult. Then, it's done."

When my older son, Matt, was a senior in high school, he wasn't getting the offers he wanted to play college football. I had taken him to a motivational seminar when he was twelve years old where he wrote, "My goal: to play college football and get a Division I scholarship." But it looked like it wasn't going to happen. I was very frustrated, and Matt was very unhappy; we thought his dream was done.

Then God gave me an idea: send the young man to prep school in my home state of Connecticut to get more exposure on a better team. His first game was fantastic game, and I thought maybe he was going to have a comeback.

I couldn't go to all his games since I was in Virginia, but a few games after his first one, I went to see him play again. My dad and I were sitting with some of the parents, including one whose son had just signed with Notre Dame. Everyone was excited, and there was another father like me whose son was hoping to get a scholarship. In a period of just three plays, I saw my son run for an eighty-five-yard touchdown, get the ball again, score another touchdown, and then score again on a two-point conversion. The other dad turned to me and said, "I think if you take that film, your son will get a scholarship." Sure enough, that film was exactly what fulfilled my son's dream, and he went on to West Point to play football for Army.

God has such marvelous plans for you. God has a great comeback for your life. God does things even when the situation looks grim. God has a way of launching us from setbacks into comebacks. I know so many people who have come back from the premature birth of a baby, from financial problems, or from divorce. Comebacks are real and can happen in your life. I trust that hope has begun to be birthed in you.

TWO REFLECTIONS ON SETBACKS

As I have gotten older and lived a little bit of life, there are two insights I've gained about setbacks. The first is, when I was younger, setbacks upset me much more than they do now. In fact, the younger I was, the more setbacks bothered me, and the older I have become, the less they bother me. I think the reason why is because I know God does great comebacks.

The second insight is that the less successful I was, the more setbacks bothered me, and the more success I've had, the less setbacks bother me. The more success you have, the more you understand there is much more success out there for you. The less success you have, especially when you're just starting out or just trying to break through, it bothers you a lot more. Some of the setbacks I had earlier in my life in my ministry and my career were upsetting to me, very upsetting. The setbacks still bother me, but I now have a better perspective, which is found in 1 Corinthians 2:9:

> But, it is just as the scriptures say. What God has planned for people who love him is more than eyes have seen or ears have heard. It has never even entered our minds.

Memorize that Scripture. Reflect or meditate on it. God has marvelous plans for you, and they're greater than your mind can conceive. I love that Scripture because I can dream up some pretty good stuff, and the Bible says God has plans even greater than we can dream ourselves.

DROP THE SETBACK MENTALITY

God wants you to have a life-changing comeback, but there are specific steps you must take.

The first step is you must drop the setback mentality, a phrase coined by my long-time friend, Tim Storey, who has coached many people, including celebrities, into comebacks. I think "setback mentality" is a good description of what can happen to a person who has a setback.

What is a setback mentality?

A setback mentality is when you're self-absorbed. You are preoccupied with your setback and the problems it has created. That preoccupation keeps you from moving forward into your comeback. You must get rid of the setback mentality, as it will have you thinking that everyone else—and this is really important—is somehow aware of your setback.

People who have a setback mentality think that everyone else sees them as a failure. Of course, that is not what everyone thinks; in fact, it is what very few people think. And those few people who do, you should not acknowledge. Once you have your comeback, those people will be the biggest haters.

So lose the setback mentality. Do not allow yourself to keep playing the setback over and over in your mind.

Have you ever noticed how certain companies or teams have remarkable comebacks or turnarounds, and it appears that nothing has changed except there is a new coach or CEO? Oftentimes, very little may appear to have changed, but the mentality changed. Someone came into the situation and said, "We can have a comeback. We can turn this thing around." The setback mentality is dropped and replaced by a comeback mentality.

In order to drop the setback mentality, you must realize that setbacks are temporary, and that they don't define you. You must remember the things you have achieved. You may need to take time today to think about what you have achieved and the obstacles you have overcome. Instead of focusing on the setback, focus on your accomplishments. Get out your resume, and look at all you have done. Look at your awards, look at your degree, look at your certificates. Realize what you have accomplished in your life in many different areas. Help yourself realize that one setback, or even a series of setbacks, does not cancel your achievements and accomplishments. It's amazing how this will affect your mentality. You can't allow the setback mentality, that negative thinking, to get inside of you, because it will keep you from taking the steps toward your comeback.

God is in the redemption business,
The restoration business,

The reconciliation business.

When you link yourself with God, when you allow Jesus Christ to come into your life and the power of the Holy Spirit to work through you, it is amazing what you can do.

The first step toward a comeback happens when you leave the setback mentality behind.

EXIT SURVIVAL MODE

You have to take another step: exit survival mode. Some have been in survival mode for far too long.

I had lunch not long ago with someone who has had some incredible setback experiences: a loss of a loved one and a financial setback. As I was talking with this person, he said that last year he kind of just checked out. That phrase "checked out" really hit me. I think that when people check out, they are in survival mode. You may need to be in survival mode for awhile to heal, but that can only be a temporary place.

There comes a point when after you've checked out, licked your wounds, and got your bearings, you have to exit survival mode. You can't stay there. You may think you need to stay in that season longer, but it is a dangerous for your comeback. You can get comfortable in survival mode because it can be quite a pity party where you dwell on how you've been wronged, how things are not fair, or how things haven't gone your way. As I said to the person I had lunch with, "It's time to get out of that. It's time for your comeback." That individual agreed that it was time to get out of survival mode and get back in the game. Injuries happen, and when they do, you heal, and you play again.

I had a weightlifting accident years ago doing a closed-grip bench press. Usually in a bench press, you hold the bar the width of your shoulders, but if you want to get a certain strength, you put your hands close together. But you don't have the same control when you lift like that, and I did it without anyone spotting me. When I put the bar back up, I heard the clank, indicating the bar was set. Only it had set on one side, not the other. As I was getting off the bench, the bar and all the weight came down on my face, breaking my orbital bone among other injuries. After I healed from that injury, it was not easy going back into the weight room. But I had to overcome that in order to get back to working out.

There comes a point when your comeback must begin, but it can't when you are in survival mode. Survival mode is a fruitless way to live.

There is no growth,
no progress, and
no impact in survival mode.

You will never become who God created you to be, nor will you experience the marvelous plans God has for your life as long as you stay in survival mode. God did not put you on this earth just to survive; God put you here to thrive. And

God wants you to thrive in the life He has for you; in the gifts, talents, and opportunities he's given you. He wants you to overcome the setback, to break through the obstacles that stand in your way.

Former Army Staff Sergeant Dan Nevins knows about overcoming obstacles and making a comeback. He lost a leg when injured in combat. Six years later, he walks without a hitch in his gait. He skis and has even climbed Mount Kilimanjaro. Nevins finds great joy in walking into a military hospital with his artificial limb under his pants. He will strike up a conversation with soldiers who are learning to deal with an amputation and show them there is nothing they can't do.

Survival mode is a very isolated way of living. The checking out can mean a lot of alone time. Now there is value in a season of reflection and introspection, but you need to reconnect with friends and get back into the swing of life. If you are going to have the comeback God wants for you, you must take the step out of survival mode and into a place of expectation for what God wants to do in your life.

RESTART YOUR DREAM ENGINE

Another step that will lead to your comeback is to restart your dream engine.

I live in NASCAR country, in fact we have one of their tracks in Richmond. I like going to those races, especially when they announce, "Gentlemen, start your engines," and those engines create an incredible sound you not only hear but feel. When those eight-hundred horsepower cars start driving around the track, it is quite a sound. And when you have had a setback, your dream engine will need to be restarted.

Setbacks do not control your life. *You* control your life.

You decide that you are going to dream again. You've had a setback; it happens to the best of us. Peyton Manning, the record-setting quarterback of the Indianapolis Colts, had neck surgery in the off-season, but he never thought he would miss any playing time. Three neck surgeries later, he ended up missing the entire 2011 NFL season. One of the greatest quarterbacks in NFL history, known for his incredible durability, has experienced quite a setback. His team suffered through a terrible losing season without him, but I have no doubt he will restart the team next season and lead them to a comeback.

You can decide that you are going to restart your dream engine; that you are not going to allow your dreams to falter and go away. I love seeing dreams fulfilled. I think it is a powerful thing when God works in someone's life in such a way that He begins to fulfill his or her dreams.

You've got to ask for God's blessing and help. Many miss out on God's blessings that come only when you ask. Simply put, a blessing is God's supernatural favor, which comes to those who ask for it. There comes a point when you decide to ask for your dreams to be fulfilled and will not allow the setback to define you anymore. You determine to move forward into the dream God has for you.

Joseph was one of the first great dreamers in the Bible. He had an incredible dream, and his own brothers tried to kill him to stop the dream from happening. They were the original haters. They didn't like that their little brother had bigger dreams than they had. There will always be people in your life who try to steal your dreams, who try to distract you from your dreams. There will always be people who will put down your dreams, who will try to discourage you from your comeback. My advice to you as a spiritual leader, a motivational speaker, and someone who has seen many dreams come true is, do not listen to those people!

When you are young, you have dreams, and occasionally older adults, because of their own disappointments and setbacks, will try to talk you out of them and make you lower your expectations. But do not allow that to happen. Even well-meaning people who care about you and have more life experience may attempt to dissuade you.

Many times, the one thing that older, more experienced people will tell younger people is that the finances will not be there. But I want you to know that it is amazing how God provides. So don't let anyone tell you that finances should hold you back from your dream. I have experienced how God provides finances in both my personal life and my ministry. Many of my dreams have been fulfilled as God both guided and provided. If you really believe God has given you this dream and is leading you, you should move in that direction. Remember, God is pro-vision.

The question for you should be, "What is next? Not what's happened, but what is next?" What does your comeback look like to you? It may be launching a new project. It may be trying a new approach. Take direct, specific action in movement toward your dream. You've had setbacks. You've learned from them. You're ready for the comeback. You understand the components of that comeback. Now it is time to start taking the steps. It is not enough to have information. It is time to act. Act from the information and knowledge you now have.

God has a great comeback in store for you!

CHAPTER 6

MR. COMEBACK

Frank Reich is a former football player. More specifically, he was a quarterback who played in both college and the NFL. His unique distinction is that he is known as Mr. Comeback because he led one of the greatest college football comebacks of all time and one of the greatest pro football comebacks of all time. In fact, he is the only person who is named *twice* in *ESPN's* list of the Twenty Greatest Sports Comebacks.

Frank is an expert on sports comebacks, but he has insights into comebacks of all kinds. I had the opportunity to interview him about comebacks.

> **Rick**: Let's go back to your college career for a moment. You are at the University of Maryland. Tell us about that comeback when you were losing to the University of Miami 31–0. What was that game like, and how did that comeback happen?

Frank: I had spent four years backing up Boomer Esiason, who was a very good quarterback and had a successful pro career. So Boomer graduates, and now I get a chance to be the starter. Well then I got hurt, separated my shoulder, and was out for a number of weeks. We're playing Miami, and we're down thirty-one points, and I had not had a chance to play in the game. I was healthy, but the coach said he didn't want to make another change at QB. I had waited all this time for my chance to play, and then I got hurt. The one thing I really wanted more than anything was taken away from me, and now that I'm ready to come back, the coach won't let me play. We're losing 31–0 at half, and coach comes in the locker room and says, "All right, Frank, you are in the second half."

To be honest, I wasn't thinking, "Hey, we're going to come back and win the game." I was just thinking one play at a time. Let's just go out there and execute the offense, one play at a time. And at the end of the day, that's one of the really big lessons I've learned about comebacks. When the circumstances, when the scoreboard, whether it's life or football, seem overwhelmingly against you, the lesson

I've learned repeatedly is one play at a time, one day at a time.

Rick: So to go from a setback to a comeback does not happen overnight; it's a process. And whether it is football, finances, your marriage, your job, or your health, it is going to be a step-by-step, day-by-day process.

Frank: I agree one hundred percent. I was very blessed to have grown up in a great family. I can remember one story. I'm a little boy, and my dad sends me out in the backyard with a wheelbarrow and a shovel. And he tells me that before I could go out and play with my friends, I have to move this pile of dirt basically across the yard. It was like two dump truck loads, I mean it was huge, and I was just nine or ten years old. I told my dad I could not do it. I went back and forth throughout the day to my dad, and every time I would complain, he would say, "Frank, one shovel full at a time, one wheelbarrow full at a time." The lesson I learned that day, which I think was part of the foundation for this game, was there was a mountain of dirt to be moved one shovel at a time. Many times, I think we look for that instantaneous moment where life can just be completely turned around. And sometimes that does happen. But a lot of times—for me most of the time—it's been one shovel full at a time, one decision at a time.

Rick: I think all of us want the miracle. We want the instant healing from the physical problem or the instant financial blessing so that we're out of the woods. But it mostly happens in a different way. God can do anything, but He usually takes you step-by-step. Let's go back to the Maryland game. So you get in the game with Miami. What happens?

Frank: I start the second half, and I don't remember exactly, but its three or four plays, and we hit a touchdown pass. Now another thing I have learned about a comeback, and this is one of the great things about football, is it's not just one guy. Okay, we scored a touchdown, but if our defense doesn't now go out there and stop them, it's all for naught. And so our defense goes and stops them, and then the next thing, we score another quick touchdown. And all of a sudden, where it seemed like we had no chance now, maybe we do. You could feel the momentum, but again it was just one play at a time. We were executing a run here, making a pass there, and the defense was playing well. You could feel the people in the stands saying, "What's going on here?"

Rick: Let's talk about momentum. I think every comeback has to have momentum. And it's amazing how momentum can almost make you better than you are. When you have it, it's the greatest thing you could have in your life. What is it like when you have the momentum and the other team does not?

Frank: Well, it's huge. I think for me my experience has been that momentum has a foundation, and the foundation is your preparation, your previous battles, and your previous journey. It is my childhood while growing up. It's the teammates, it's the practice, it's all that stuff going in that prepares you for the moment in time when momentum is there. Can you capitalize on it? Can you take that step? Can you throw that pass? Can you make the right decision?

Rick: Tell us about your preparation. Tell us a little bit about how you grew up in Pennsylvania.

Frank: My mom and dad were high school teachers. My dad was a football coach. But my dad was one of those coaches who never forced me to play. He didn't even tell me when football tryouts were. I had to find out from my buddies. One time when I was snooping around like a ten- or eleven-year-old boy will do, I found these big paper bags in my parent's closet, and I pulled them out. I had never seen them before, and there were two big scrapbooks. I discovered that my dad was the captain of the Penn State football team. He was an All–American, and I never even knew this!

Rick: Wow.

Frank: So my dad comes home, and I said, "Dad, what's the deal here?" He said, "I never wanted you to feel like you had to play football if you didn't want to." He was just a great role model for me, a great example. He loved me unconditionally. So when I started playing, I never really felt the pressure from my dad. I felt like he was going to love me and support me whether I was a good football player or a terrible football player. His one rule was you give one hundred percent to whatever you do, and if you start a season, you finish a season.

Rick: So part of a comeback is keeping focused on where you want to get to and not giving up for any reason. Not allowing the many distractions in life to keep you from your goal.

Frank: Absolutely.

Rick: So how do you end up going to Maryland instead of Penn State if your dad was at Penn State?

Frank: Excellent question. Penn State recruited me, but Penn State also had a reputation for taking high school quarterbacks and making them into linebackers. I knew that I couldn't play any other position other than quarterback, so I went to Maryland. I just kind of felt like Maryland was the right place for me.

Rick: When you get there, one of the best quarterbacks to play the game, Boomer Esiason, ends up being on your team, and so you have to wait your turn.

Frank: Yeah, we ended up being the best man in each other's weddings. So here I am competing against this guy, sitting on the bench behind him, but yet we're real close friends.

Rick: And then you both ended up playing in the NFL.

Frank: Yes.

Rick: So finish out the Miami game for me. The defense is doing its job. The O line's doing its job. Did Miami ever even score again?

Frank: They scored one time late. In fact, it was 31–0 at half. Then we got to the point where we were up 42–31, and they kick a field goal somewhere in the second half, so it was now 42–34. They actually got the ball back and scored to make it 42–40 with just a couple minutes to go. They go for the two-point conversion and have a chance to tie the game, and we stop them.

Rick: And that is how you won the game. You scored forty-two points in one half of football.

Frank: Yes. That was the comeback.

Rick: Wow. So then how did you get in the NFL?

Frank: I only ended up starting six games in my entire college career. And yet I was drafted by the Buffalo Bills in the third round. I was sitting in my college room with my girlfriend, who's now my wife, waiting for that phone call on draft day. I knew I wasn't going to be a high draft pick, but they told me I'd probably be drafted somewhere in the second or third round, and I was the first player taken in the third round. We weren't engaged, but we had been dating for like four years. I think we both knew at that point that we would get married and this was going to be our life. We had decided that it was going to be great to play in the NFL anywhere. Her words were, "I just pray it's anywhere but the Buffalo Bills." So I get that phone call. I pick up the phone, and the man said, "This is Kay Stephenson, the head coach of the Buffalo Bills." I was thinking, "You got to be kidding me!" And she was in the background going, "Who is it? Who is it?" And I go, "It's Buffalo!" She started crying.

Rick: Okay. So you get to Buffalo.

Frank: There were two or three guys on that team that I ended up becoming close with who had a big impact on my life. So I thank God he took us to Buffalo.

Rick: Tell me about the Oilers game, because the game is legendary. It is one thing to have a comeback in the regular season, and it is another thing in the playoffs. Just take us into the pregame, the team mentality, and then as the game progresses.

Frank: Well, what most people don't know is in the last week of the regular NFL season, we played the Houston Oilers at Houston. If we won that game, we were going to get a bye. The short story is Jim Kelly got hurt in that game. I came in, played really badly, and we lost 28–3. As a result of losing, we now don't get a bye, and we play the Oilers again the next week. Because they beat up on us the first time, now everything in the media is that the Oilers have the momentum.

Rick: Jim Kelly, the All-Pro QB, is hurt, and you played a terrible game the previous week.

Frank: Yes, Kelly is hurt, I played poorly, and people were not giving us a chance. Then we come out in the first half, and Warren Moon is lighting it up, and they are winning 28–3 at halftime. Now do the math. If they beat us 28–3 the week before, and now they are beating us 28–3 again, cumulatively it is 56–6.

Rick: That is bad.

Frank: Oh, it gets worse. We get the ball to start the second half, and I throw an interception that is returned for a touchdown on my first pass. So that now makes it 35–3.

Rick: Did you say, "Guys, don't worry. I've done this before"?

Frank: No.

Rick: You did not say that?

Frank: No, I did not say that. Because the Maryland-Miami game was a big game, and there were guys on the sidelines who knew. I do think that was a factor for me at least in the game.

Rick: You had confidence.

Frank: The confidence to know if we're going to come back from thirty-two points, it doesn't all happen at once. It's going to take everybody on this team, and we've just got to execute one play at a time.

Rick: By your own admission, you did not play well in that final regular season game. You didn't really play that well in the first half.

Frank: Yeah, that's right.

Rick: How do you have confidence for the comeback with those kinds of setbacks? How do you restore your confidence?

Frank: It is a matter of preparation. There is a great quote that I remember from a famous general. He is talking to his men before they go into battle, and he says, "You know, you can determine the manner of man you will be whenever and wherever you get called into action. Because no man becomes suddenly different from his habit and cherished thought." I do believe that extraordinary things happen when ordinary people maintain a consistency, have a belief, and have some conviction.

Rick: So confidence is important.

Frank: It is really important. But I've learned through football that some of the times I find confidence in my greatest humiliations and being down that low, and then realizing I'm not in control. That it takes teammates; it takes a whole team for something like this to happen. It takes support.

Rick: So how did you do it? How did you have such an incredible comeback?

Frank: So it was 35–3. We go down, and we have a pretty quick score, and now it's 35–10. We then have the surprise onside kick. That was really one of those great calls by our head coach. To be thinking that far in advance that if there is going to be a comeback, we're going to have to take a chance and do something out of the ordinary. It was a great call by our head coach, Marv Levy, and we executed it perfectly. That call really kind of ignited something in our team. Three plays later, I throw a touchdown pass to Don Beebe. Warren Moon throws an interception. A few plays later, I throw another touchdown pass. Now it is 35–24. Only like six minutes had gone by in the game, and everybody is like, "Wow!"

Rick: Now it is a game, and there is plenty of time left.

Frank: There is plenty of time left. And we just kind of kept rolling. Between each series, I'm over on the sidelines, pacing back and forth, humming the words to the song "In Christ Alone" that my sister had called me that week and told me about. If you want to have a comeback, you can come part way back and then all of a sudden get caught up in the excitement and the momentum. You have got to stay doing what you've been doing that got you there. And we did get there because we ended up going into overtime, where we won on a field goal. So we came back from the biggest deficit in NFL playoff history.

Rick: Right.

Frank: So part of the way I stayed focused was just kind of humming that song, because the words gave me a quiet confidence. Not that God was going to be on my side and everything was going to work out how I wanted it, but it just gave me a quiet confidence. And that is why after the game was over at the press conference I quoted that song.

Rick: Because it was that significant.

Frank: Yes.

Rick: Tell me about your faith and your spiritual journey. Where did it all start?

Frank: Well, as God has it sometimes, he takes ordinary people in ordinary circumstances. I was involved in football a lot. I grew up in football, so football was primary in my life. I waited, backed up Boomer Esiason for four years, and then when I finally get my chance, I get hurt, and now everything is taken away from me. My dream of playing in the NFL is gone. I recover from my injury, but now the guy who took my place had been playing well, and the coach isn't going to let me play. I'm done. It's over.

Rick: At twenty-two years old.

Frank: Yeah. I mean, for me, it's over. I can laugh at that now, but when you are twenty-two, and this is your life, it is real. Football was everything to me, and I thought it was taken away. There was a minister on campus with Campus Crusade for Christ who had been kind of telling me some things. My girlfriend, who is now my wife, was telling me things in my other ear, "You know, Frank, you need to kind of just think through this and get your priorities straight and think about your relationship with the Lord." So it was in those moments in college, going through that difficult time, that I said, "Okay, God. You got my attention. I'm giving my life to you. I'm surrendering my life to you. Forgive me of my sin. And, Jesus, I do believe you are who you say you are, and I'm going to commit my life to following you."

Rick: So then where does it go from there?

Frank: I'm kind of wallowing around. I'm at chapel on Sundays, and then I'm out in the bars doing my own thing early on in my

Christian days. My life really hadn't changed a whole lot, but a little bit. God was very gracious to put some really strong men in my life, including a team chaplain. He invited me to start coming to Bible study and getting involved.

Rick: So you have a nice long career in the NFL.

Frank: Yes, fourteen years. One other really quick note about the comeback game that I think is important. After our comeback game, we are playing in Super Bowl XXVII against the Cowboys. Jim Kelly had started that game. When I came into the game, we were losing 17–7, and I'm thinking, "We're going to come back and win this game." A month before, we were down by thirty-two, now we're only down by ten. I quoted that song after that game. Now God's going to bless me with a Super Bowl victory, and I might even be the MVP!

Rick: Wow! Okay.

Frank: Well, the long story short is that we lost 52–17. I am a Super Bowl record holder—I hold the record for the most fumbles in a Super Bowl game. And I threw a couple interceptions too, by the way. So it wasn't just the fumbles. So in a course of one month, I go from the highest of highest to the lowest of the lowest. But the lesson through that is being consistent.

Rick: There are lessons to be learned from setbacks and from comebacks. Your stories are fantastic; they are an encouragement and an inspiration. Thank you, Frank.

CHAPTER 7

TOP TEN GREATEST COMEBACKS OF ALL TIME

In choosing ten comebacks as the greatest of all time, some standard was necessary for arriving at such an auspicious list. My criteria involved two elements, and within each element, a measurement was used. The elements were the nature of the setback and the prominence of the comeback. The measurement for each was simply the greatness of the span between the setback and the comeback.

There have been many great comebacks in history. This book is devoted to the concept that there can be many more. But there are certain comebacks that simply stand apart from all others because of their greatness. My top ten list begins with number ten.

ROBERT DOWNEY JR.

Robert Downey Jr. had a great amount of success at a young age. He starred in a number of films throughout the 1980s and 1990s, receiving an Academy Award nomination for best actor in the 1992 film, *Chaplin*.

After this promising start, Robert began to face problems in his personal life. From 1996–2001, he was arrested numerous times on drug-related charges. In April 1996, he was arrested for possession of cocaine, marijuana, and an unloaded .357 magnum while speeding down Sunset Boulevard. He was sentenced to three years' probation and required to undergo mandatory drug testing.

But that first arrest did not stop his destructive behavior. A year later, he missed a court-ordered drug test and had to spend four months in the Los Angeles County jail. Even jail time failed to change Robert's behavior, and in 1999, he missed another drug test and was sentenced to three years at the California Substance Abuse Treatment Facility and State Prison in Corcoran, California. He received a big break when he was unexpectedly released early for previous time served in 1996.

Unfortunately, Robert's addiction was too strong, and he was arrested yet again the following year for possession of cocaine and Valium. In July 2001, he pleaded no contest to the charges but avoided jail time because of California's Proposition 36, which was aimed at helping nonviolent drug offenders to overcome addiction through court-ordered rehabilitation.

Downey told Oprah in 2004 that he finally decided he needed help and reached out for it. He said, "You can reach out for help in a kind of half-assed way, and you'll get it, and you won't take advantage of it. It's not that difficult to overcome these seemingly ghastly problems … what's hard is to decide to actually do it." After five years of setbacks, he decided he was going to have a comeback.

While he managed to stay employed with small projects throughout his battle with drug addiction, it was in 2008 when his career comeback solidified. He was nominated for Best Supporting Actor for his role in *Tropic Thunder*. He landed the lead role in the movie *Iron Man*, and *Entertainment Weekly* named him "Entertainer of the Year." In addition, *Time* named him one of the 100 Most Influential People of 2008.

Robert now has the lead role in two widely successful movie franchises, *Iron Man* and *Sherlock Holmes*. In 2010, his role as Sherlock Holmes earned him a Golden Globe for Best Performance by an Actor in a Motion Picture. Downey is one of the most popular and sought-after actors in Hollywood, solidifying his comeback. He has also started a foundation to help others.

JOSH HAMILTON

Josh Hamilton was the first overall pick in the 1999 Major League Baseball draft by the Tampa Bay Devil Rays, receiving a $3.96 million dollar signing bonus. He was an unlikely candidate as a future drug addict, but unfortunately, adversity struck his life and young career in the form of numerous injuries.

In 2001, Josh was involved in a car accident that placed him on injured reserve. In his first three seasons, he missed a total of 236 games because of injuries. During this time, he self-medicated with drugs and alcohol. As a result, he tested positive for substance abuse, was suspended, and put into a treatment program.

However, this did not stop his addictive behavior. In 2004, Major League Baseball suspended him indefinitely for violating the joint drug treatment and prevention program. At this point, he had become a full-blown addict; the substance abuse as a coping mechanism for his injuries and that stalled his promising career had become the agent of his career destruction. His depression worsened.

Finally, in 2005, he hit rock bottom, waking up on his grandmother's doorstep after what would be his final crack cocaine binge. Hamilton had experienced a gigantic setback, and his future was very dim.

He chose a road that led to recovery and his comeback in baseball. In an *ESPN* article about his story, Josh describes his comeback, "It's a God thing. It's the only possible explanation." In that same article, he describes two dreams that encompassed his journey back from addiction:

I was fighting the Devil, an awful-looking thing. I had a stick or a bat or something and every time I hit the Devil, he'd fall and get back up. Over and over I hit him, until I was exhausted, and he was still standing.

> I woke up in a sweat, as if I'd been truly fighting, and the terror that gripped me makes that dream feel real to this day. I'd been alone for so long, alone with the fears and emotions I worked so hard to kill. I'm not embarrassed to admit that after I woke up that night, I walked down the hall to my grandmother's room and crawled under the covers with her. The Devil stayed out of my dreams for seven months after that. I stayed clean and worked hard and tried to put my marriage and my life back together. I got word in June 2006 that I'd been reinstated by Major League Baseball, and a few weeks afterward, the Devil reappeared.

> It was the same dream, with an important difference. I would hit him, and he would bounce back up, the ugliest and most hideous creature you could imagine. This devil seemed

unbeatable; I couldn't knock him out. But just when I felt like giving up, I felt a presence by my side. I turned my head and saw Jesus, battling alongside me. We kept fighting, and I was filled with strength. The Devil didn't stand a chance.

You can doubt me, but I swear to you I dreamed it. When I woke up, I felt at peace. I wasn't scared. To me, the lesson was obvious: Alone, I couldn't win this battle. With Jesus, I couldn't lose.

Josh's reinstatement was just the beginning of his remarkable comeback. In 2008, he was selected to his first All-Star team, where he also participated in the Home Run Derby, setting an opening round record of twenty-eight home runs and finishing with the second most home runs of all time in Derby history with thirty-five. His Home Run Derby explosion introduced Josh to the public in a big way, furthering his comeback.

Josh has been selected to the All-Star team for three straight years (2009–2011.) In 2010, he won several single-season honors in the American League, including the batting title, ALCS MVP, and most impressively, MVP of the entire American League.

The man who almost lost his life and career to addiction has now become one of baseball's biggest stars. In addition to his personal success, he has led his team, the Texas Rangers, who had never won an American League pennant, to the past two American League pennants (2010–2011) and World Series appearances.

Josh's comeback is still continuing. Only in time will his full success be known.

ULYSSES S. GRANT

Grant was both a general and a president. He was an American hero in the truest sense of the word. Misunderstood by many people who don't know his whole story, his life is a powerful example of a comeback.

Grant was the son of a tanner in Ohio and was soft-spoken and easily embarrassed. He went to West Point and entered into the army as an officer. He served in the Mexican-American War and then was sent to the new Oregon territory out west. He did not like it; he did not like the climate, and he did not like being separated from his wife and children. In his depression, he drank too much, quit the army, gave up his officer commission, and went back home.

Grant tried his hand at a couple of different things and failed at both real estate and business. He was working in his family's tannery, making very little money, when the Civil War broke out. The Union Army contacted him since he was a West Point graduate and had combat experience in the Mexican-American War and asked to rejoin the army, which he did.

He actually did not do well in his first battle, but then he had a great victory at Fort Donaldson, and then he won a big battle at Shiloh, which got the attention of President Lincoln. Lincoln kept going through generals, trying to find somebody who actually would get the job done, and he decided that Grant was someone who would actually fight.

Grant kept getting promoted until he was the top general of all the Union forces. He won the Civil War not by fancy maneuvers or clever strategy but by confronting the Confederate Army in the field and defeating it. The man with the rumpled uniform, unkempt beard, and ever-present cigar accepted the surrender from General Lee of the Confederate forces at Appomattox.

Grant was then elected as president of the United States. In fact, he was reelected twice, serving two terms as president. Though his two terms were riddled with political and financial scandals (none directly involving him), he managed to bring a calming influence to the country and bring peace between the North and South and between the US and the rest of the world.

The culmination of Grant's comeback was his memoirs that he wrote after he left the presidency. He wrote *Memoirs* a book about his life which at the time became the best-selling book in American history, excluding the Bible. The shy boy from humble beginnings who failed at much in the early part of his life had an incredible comeback. He was the top general that lead the Union's victory in the Civil War, was elected president for two terms of the United States, and wrote the best-selling book of all time.

KURT WARNER

Kurt Warner is a Super Bowl champion, two-time National Football League MVP, and Hall of Fame candidate. His journey to success consisted of many setbacks and two remarkable comebacks. Throughout his incredible journey, he has always given credit to his faith in Jesus Christ as the foundation for his success.

After his college football career at the University of Northern Iowa, Warner went undrafted in the 1994 NFL draft. He was invited to try out for the Green Bay Packers but was released before the start of the regular season. With no other options, he took a job working at a grocery store in Cedar Rapids, Iowa, making $5.50 an hour. He also worked as a graduate assistant coach for the Northern Iowa football program while waiting for another NFL opportunity.

No NFL team was willing to give him an opportunity, so he signed with the Arena Football League's Iowa Barnstormers in 1995. During his two seasons in the AFL (1996 and 1997), Warner was named first team All-Arena and led his team to two Arena Bowl appearances. Finally, the Saint Louis Rams signed him in 1998, but they allocated him to the NFL

Europe's Amsterdam Admirals, where he led the league in touchdowns and passing yards. After that season, he came back to the Rams as their third-string quarterback.

The 1999 season would change the course of Warner's life and career. The Rams' starting quarterback, Trent Green, tore his ACL in a preseason game, and Warner became the starter. Up to this point in his career, he had never been a starter in the NFL and had actually played very little. That year, he would have one of the all-time best single seasons by a quarterback, throwing for 4,353 yards with forty-one touchdown passes and a completion rate of 65.1%.

Warner led the Rams' high-powered offense known as the "greatest show on turf" to a Super Bowl victory over the Tennessee Titans. In that game, he threw for a Super Bowl record 414 yards and was named the Super Bowl MVP. In addition, he would become the seventh player to win both the league MVP and Super Bowl MVP in the same season.

Warner won a second league MVP in the 2001 season when he again led his team to the Super Bowl, where they lost to the Patriots. In a close game decided by three points, Warner threw for the third highest passing total in Super Bowl history.

After winning two MVPs in three seasons, Warner suffered another setback when he injured his throwing hand and did not complete the 2002 season. In 2003, he was replaced as the starter after fumbling six times in the season-opening game. He was released the next season and signed a two-year contract with the New York Giants. His setback continued as he was replaced in the middle of the season by the highly touted rookie, Eli Manning. At the end of the season, Warner decided to void the second year of his contract and become a free agent.

In 2005, Warner signed a one-year contract with the Arizona Cardinals. He started most of that season and had a good enough year that he signed a three-year extension the following year. The Cardinals then drafted quarterback Matt Leinart out of the University of Southern California, who replaced Warner in week four of the 2006 season. For the second time in his career, Warner was replaced by a rookie quarterback even though he was a two-time MVP and Super Bowl winner.

Leinart was named the starter again in 2007 but was ineffective, and Warner regained the job later in the season. Despite Warner's success, there was a quarterback controversy in the off-season. Eventually, Warner was named the starter, where he led the Cardinals to a division title, their first playoff appearance since 1998, and then the Super Bowl against the Pittsburgh Steelers. The Cardinals lost a very close game, but Warner threw for 377 yards, making him the record holder for the top three passing yard totals in Super Bowl history.

Warner retired as a four-time All-Pro, having played in three Super Bowls and thrown over one hundred touchdowns for two different teams. His outstanding play in the playoffs make him one of the best clutch players in NFL history, and his off-field accomplishments culminated in his being named the 2008 NFL Man of the Year. Twice tossed aside as not good enough to start in the NFL, Warner's comebacks are truly remarkable.

LANCE ARMSTRONG

The Lance Armstrong comeback story has been celebrated for good reason. His comeback has inspired millions of people, and his "LiveStrong" campaign in partnership with Nike has motivated thousands to overcome cancer and other challenges. The LiveStrong Foundation has raised over 325 million dollars for cancer research.

At age sixteen, Lance became a pro triathlete, and by nineteen, he had won two national sprint course triathlon championships. Then at twenty, he became the United States Amateur Cycling Champion. One year later, he won his first professional race as a member of Team Motorola, and at age twenty-one, he became the youngest cyclist to ever win the UCI Road World Championship. By twenty-five, he was one of the world's best cyclists. However, that same year, Lance was diagnosed with stage-three testicular cancer, which had spread to his lungs, abdomen, and brain.

Lance took an active role in educating himself about cancer. Armed with knowledge, support, and confidence, he undertook an aggressive treatment. After undergoing surgery to remove the diseased testicle, his doctor gave him less than a forty percent chance to live. Lance then had his brain tumors removed, and amazingly, by 1998, his cancer had gone into complete remission. Lance then began his comeback. His workouts are legendary for their difficulty, and they launched him out of his setback.

Not only did he survive cancer, but also Lance's greatest accomplishments as an athlete have come since his recovery. Before his diagnosis, he had won three stages of the Tour de France but had never won the entire race. His comeback began with a fourth place finish in a race in Spain in 1998. In 1999, he entered the Tour de France and miraculously won it just two years after cancer surgery. Although impressive, that win was just the first of seven straight races that he would win.

No one in history had ever won seven straight Tour de France titles. At that point, Lance's comeback was complete. After his final Tour de France victory in 2005, he announced his retirement.

POST-WAR GERMANY AND JAPAN

The aftermath of World War II left Germany and Japan devastated. Most of their large cities were severely damaged along with the countless lives lost. There were shortages of food and a lack of housing and transportation. In addition to all of this was the humiliation of defeat. The worldwide view of these nations was one of disdain as evil empires whose aggression had caused another world war.

Both Germany and Japan had truly experienced a national setback. Both governments and economies were completely restructured by post-war occupation from the Allied Forces. The ramifications of this left both countries in far worse shape than their prewar conditions. Their comebacks are known as the post-war economic miracle. Germany and Japan are now the third and fourth largest economies in the world, respectively.

By the end of the war, Japan had lost two million lives and over one hundred cities were destroyed. Industrial production stood at less than ten percent of its prewar level. The United States occupied Japan from 1945–1952, during which time it brought demilitarization, democratization, as well as industrial, land, and education reform.

The Korean War propelled Japan's economy into recovery, as it became the principal supplier of food and arms for the US armed forces. During this period, industry was rejuvenated, and by 1955, industrial output was back to its prewar level.

Japan began rebranding itself by abandoning militarism and focusing on becoming an industrial and technological nation. Much of modern technology (HD televisions, DVD players, audio equipment) has been invented or made in Japan. According to the Japanese economist Ryuotaro Komiya, Japan's overriding goals have been making the economy self-sufficient and catching up with the West. Japan's postal savings institution has fostered a high savings rate, reducing the cost of capital and allowing debt to be financed internally.

They have also developed a highly efficient workforce through their rigorous education system. Ultimately, from 1950–1980, Japan's economy grew at a remarkable rate of ten percent annually.

By 1948, the German people had been living under price controls for twelve years and rationing for nine. Hitler had imposed price controls for his own economic gain, resulting in severe food shortages and high inflation. The end of the war meant the end of these policies, thus unleashing industrial productivity.

In just the first six months, industrial production had increased by fifty percent. The split of Germany into the Communist East and the Democratic West in 1961 concentrated economic growth solely in the West, where it stalled from decreases in the labor force that accompanied the split.

The reunification of Germany in 1990 brought about another comeback, as there were now plentiful laborers for their various industries. At the core of Germany's successful comeback was its highly efficient industrial sector. Germany's economy now excels above all other European countries.

BUFFALO BILLS: 1993 PLAYOFF GAME

The Buffalo Bills played the Houston Oilers in an NFL playoff game in 1993, where the Bills recovered from a thirty-two-point deficit to win the game in overtime. The Bills' comeback was the greatest postseason comeback in NFL history.

The Oilers had beaten the Bills 28–3 the week before, which cost them a first-round bye in the playoffs. In the first half of the game, the Oilers continued their domination over the Bills. Quarterback Warren Moon went 19–22 for 220 passing yards and four touchdowns to put the Oilers up 28–3 at halftime. Just 1:41 into the second half, Bills quarterback Frank Reich threw an interception that was returned for a touchdown, putting the Oilers up 35–3. On top of their thirty-two-point deficit, the Bills lost their star running back, Thurman Thomas, to a hip injury.

The Oilers kicked off with a squib kick that was very poor, giving the Bills excellent field position. The Bills drove the short field and scored their first touchdown. In what may have been the turning point of the game, the Bills then tried an onside kick and were successful in recovering the ball. Just four plays later, Reich hit Don Beebe with a thirty-eight-yard touchdown pass. The Bills then forced the Oilers to punt for the first time in the game, resulting in just a twenty-five-yard punt. The Bills scored again on a touchdown pass from Reich to Andre Reed, and all of the sudden the score was 35–24.

Ten minutes into the third quarter, the Bills had scored twenty-one points and the Oilers had only run three plays for three yards. The Bills then intercepted Moon and scored on a fourth down attempt with another touchdown pass to Reed. In the fourth quarter, the Bills scored another touchdown on a pass to Reed, and now the Bills were actually ahead of the Oilers 38–35. Moon led the Oilers on a sixty-three-yard drive, resulting in a field goal that tied the score and sent the game into overtime.

The Oilers won the coin toss and could have won the game without the Bills ever even getting the ball, but Moon threw an interception. Reich led the Bills down the field, where they kicked a thirty-two-yard field goal to win the game. In just one half of a game and a little overtime, the Bills erased a thirty-two-point setback and produced the greatest comeback professional football has ever seen. And they did it in the playoffs.

BOSTON RED SOX 2004

The Boston Red Sox is one of the most famous professional sports franchises in America. Its popularity has created the Red Sox Nation, where people from all over the world, not just New England, follow them fanatically. Their fan base has grown even larger since they pulled off the greatest baseball playoff comeback in history.

The Sox had a successful beginning to their franchise, including winning the very first World Series. They went on to win four more world championships by 1918, and the future looked very bright for years to come. However, after 1918, they did not win another World Series for eighty-six years. It was called the "Curse of the Bambino" since, after they traded Babe Ruth to the hated New York Yankees, they never won another world championship. They played in four World Series but never won, even with some of the greatest baseball players ever like Ted Williams and Carl Yazstremski.

In 2004, the Sox played their rival, the New York Yankees, in the American League Championship series. They had lost to them in the same series the previous year. The Red Sox began the series by losing the first two games, and then in game three, they lost 19–8 at home, which was the worst playoff loss in Red Sox history. They were now down 3–0, and no team in Major League Baseball history had ever come back from a 3–0 deficit to win a postseason series.

Game four went into extra innings and was won by the Red Sox on a walk-off homer by David "Big Papi" Ortiz. Game five also went into extra innings and was won when Ortiz hit an RBI single. The Red now had to go back to unfriendly Yankee stadium for game six after having barely escaped in the last two games, knowing they still would lose the series if they lost one more game.

The Red Sox won game six thanks in large part to the pitching of Kurt Schilling, despite having stitches in his ankle. In game seven, for the first time, the Yankees were in danger of losing the series. Incredibly, they did lose the game *and* the series. The Boston Red Sox had overcome the greatest deficit in baseball history against their most-hated rival to have a comeback like no other in playoff baseball.

However, the comeback was not yet complete. The Sox still had to win the World Series in order to have a world championship. They played the Saint Louis Cardinals, who had won more world championships than any club except the Yankees. The Red Sox came into the series on a four-game winning streak and amazingly won four straight to sweep the Cardinals and win their first world championship in eighty-six years. The greatest baseball comeback was now complete.

ABRAHAM LINCOLN

Many (myself included) consider Lincoln to be the greatest president in the history of the United States. He led the country through its greatest moral and military crisis, essentially saved the country from destruction, and directed it toward restoration.

Lincoln grew up in meager circumstances. His mother died when he was just nine years old, and for his education, he was basically self-taught. He tried his hand at business and failed at it not once but twice. During that time, he ran for his first elected office and lost. His first true love died probably of typhoid fever, and Lincoln had what most today would call a nervous breakdown.

Though he was elected to four terms in the Illinois House of Representatives, when Lincoln ran for US Congress, he lost. He also ran twice for the US Senate and lost both times, as well as losing the election in 1856 as the vice presidential candidate. Previous to his run for the presidency, Lincoln had won only one national election in his entire political career. Although he experienced an incredible number of setbacks in both his personal and professional life, Lincoln would make one of the greatest comebacks in history.

In 1860, Lincoln was elected the sixteenth president of the United States, marking the beginning of his remarkable comeback. His presidency began with the secession of the southern states and the beginning of the Civil War at Fort Sumter. Lincoln had the immense challenge of directing the war effort, handling his normal presidential responsibilities, and dealing with the criticism of antiwar Democrats. He showed deft political skill and leadership acumen in dealing with all of his challenges.

Lincoln had many great accomplishments that solidify his place in American history and reveal the greatness of his comeback. His speech, the Gettysburg Address, is the most quoted speech in American history. The Emancipation Proclamation freed all slaves and stands as one of the greatest acts of moral leadership in history. His reelection in 1864 confirmed that his continued leadership was vital to the country, and his approach and attitude toward the defeated southern states helped reunite the nation.

Without Lincoln, the United States would look very different today. Considering his many setbacks, what he accomplished mark his comeback as one of the greatest of all time.

JESUS CHRIST'S RESURRECTION

Jesus was the most important person who ever lived. His life, death, and resurrection literally changed the course of human history, experiencing the ultimate setback and the ultimate comeback.

Jesus began his life miraculously, having been born of a virgin. Conceived by the Holy Spirit through the Virgin Mary, Jesus was literally both God and man. Jesus was unique, which was recognized by the religious scholars of his day when he was still young.

Jesus launched his public ministry when he was thirty years old. He overcame the temptation of the Devil in the desert, proclaimed himself to be the Messiah, and gathered together a team of twelve disciples. He traveled throughout his region performing good works, healing the sick, and teaching God's message. He performed many miracles and created quite a stir amongst many religious leaders. Jesus predicted that the kingdom of God would come, but it would not be an earthly kingdom or a political revolution. Rather, Jesus would become the leader of each individual's life and establish his teachings as the way to live. Many chose to become Jesus' followers, and he gained great popularity with the general public.

Jesus lived a perfect, sinless life. However, the religious leaders of his day viewed him with suspicion and disdain and convinced one of Jesus' disciples to betray him. Jesus was then arrested and brought before the Roman authorities for punishment. Pilate the Roman governor did not think Jesus was guilty of anything but gave them a choice. They demanded that Jesus receive the death sentence.

Jesus was guilty of no crime and had done incredible good, yet he was crucified, the most painful and horrendous death in the ancient world. His hands and feet were nailed to intersecting wooden beams, which were then lifted up and placed in the ground. In order for Jesus to breathe, he had to lift himself up, tearing His flesh in the process. Every moment on the cross, Jesus was in excruciating pain and was mocked, ridiculed, and spat upon. Jesus also had a crown of thorns placed on His head and His side was pierced with a sword. Finally, Jesus died. There can be no greater setback than to be cruelly and mercilessly killed.

Jesus died on a Friday. Some women went to the cave where he was buried on Sunday morning and found the stone in the front of the tomb rolled away. Jesus was not dead but had risen from the grave! The greatest comeback in history had taken place. A dead person had come back to life; death had been beaten. Jesus then appeared to His disciples and explained to them what had happened.

Jesus died as a sinless person for all the sins of humanity, and his resurrection proved his victory over sin and death. Anyone who confesses their sins to Jesus will be forgiven and granted eternal life. Thus, because of Jesus' comeback, any person can have their greatest personal comeback.

The setback of mistakes, failures, and sins can be forgiven. The comeback of inner peace, purpose, and meaning in life is now available. We can live our lives in a personal relationship with God, experience his plan for our lives, and spend eternity in heaven with him after this life is over. Thanks to Jesus, life's greatest comeback is available to you any time you choose.

Author Bio

Rick McDaniel is the founder/senior pastor of Richmond Community Church in Richmond, Virginia. The church is known for its contemporary style and innovative services and has a worldwide reach through its Internet Campus (www.highimpactchurch.tv.) Rick's messages are featured in video form on www.lightsource.com and in audio form on www.oneplace.com, as well as on Audible and Amazon.

Rick has earned three degrees, including an advanced degree from Duke University. He has traveled and spoken on five continents and has authored three previous books. Rick has been married for twenty-nine years to his wife, Michelle, and they have two sons, Matt and Wes.

For More Information:

www.rickmcdaniel.com

www.highimpactliving.com

http://twitter.com/rickmcdaniel

www.facebook.com/highimpactchurch

CPSIA information can be obtained at www.ICGtesting.com
Printed in the USA
BVOW011848180312

285409BV00002B/1/P